CW01188386

The Night before Christmas
or A Visit from St. Nicholas

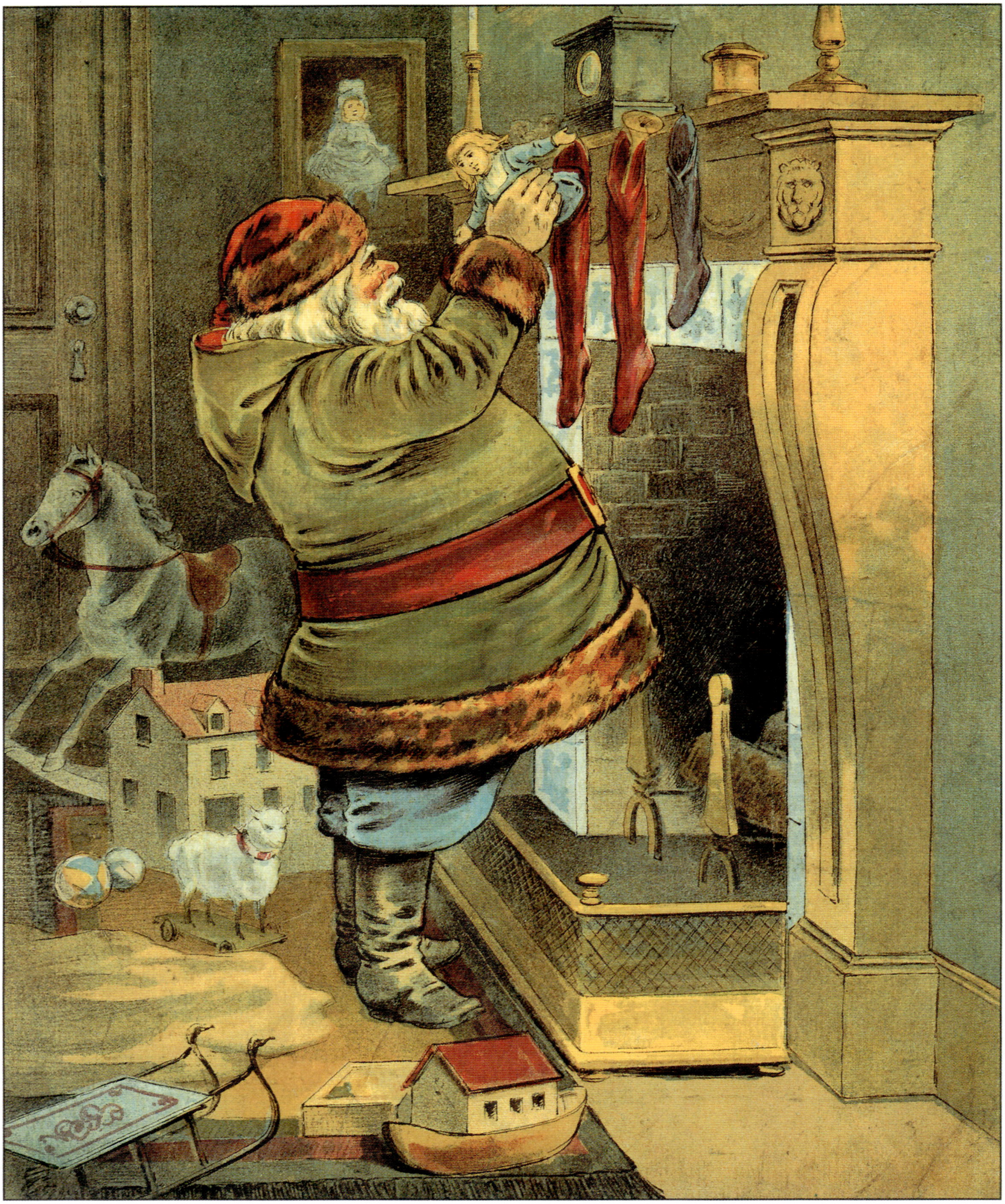

The Night before Christmas
or a Visit from St. Nicholas

CLEMENT CLARKE MOORE

AN ANTIQUE REPRODUCTION

ARCTURUS

INTRODUCTION

*'Twas the night before Christmas, when all through the house
Not a creature was stirring, not even a mouse…*

These may be some of the most famous opening lines of any festive verse, yet this couplet, and the poem that follows, are more than just a jaunty rhyme to keep little ones quiet at Christmas time. They have helped to shape the modern Christmas, with its tradition of gifts delivered by Santa and his flying reindeer.

The poem was indeed written to entertain children. It was penned in 1822 by Clement Clarke Moore (1779–1863) as a gift to his own family, supposedly on his return journey from a Christmas shopping trip. However, it was not intended for publication. It was only a year later, when a friend submitted it to the *New York Sentinel*, that it came into general circulation. Even then, it was published anonymously. Moore was a serious scholar and professor of religion, and it is said that he wished to remain distant from a piece of verse for children. He eventually claimed ownership in 1844 when his children persuaded him to include the rhyme in a book of his poetry.

The tale is notable for its description of St. Nicholas as a jolly old man with twinkling eyes and rosy cheeks. This vision of a character who personifies Christmas helped fire the imaginations of illustrators such as Thomas Nast and, in this beautifully decorated edition, William Roger Snow. They seized upon the main character's elf-like appearance, his little round belly, and his general merry demeanor. The poem also offers rich illustrative pickings with the eight reindeer soaring over the rooftops with a sleigh full of presents behind them.

For centuries, Old Father Christmas had brought good cheer in the midwinter, spreading kindness and happiness rather than gifts and toys. He was often dressed in green (as a symbol of the forthcoming spring) or cozy furs to protect him from the harsh winter weather. Now, enraptured listeners were given a vision of a merry fellow who flew from house to house, dropping down chimneys to leave toys in the stockings pinned up by children the evening before. Moore includes eight miniature reindeer, each joyfully named, with nods to the northern European traditions of Sinterklaas who had a big, red book in which he kept records of which children had behaved well through the year.

The English artist William Roger Snow (1834–1907) draws upon his contemporary Victorian influences here, showing the busy preparation in the workshop in the run-up to Christmas, with St. Nicholas getting the gifts ready for delivery to his long list of boys and girls. Snow was a prolific illustrator—and author—of both children's and adult's literature. He also worked under the aliases Clifford Merton and Richard André, and illustrated other children's classics including *Puss in Boots, Jack and the Beanstalk,* and *Red Riding Hood.*

His delightful depiction of Moore's jolly St. Nick will add even more enjoyment to the reading of this classic poem, and give rise to sweet dreams once those sleepy heads eventually hit the pillow on Christmas Eve.

"THE NIGHT BEFORE CHRISTMAS."

"ALL SNUG IN THEIR BEDS."

A Visit from St. Nicholas

'Twas the night before Christmas,
            when all through the house
Not a creature was stirring,
            not even a mouse;
The stockings were hung by the chimney with care,
In hopes that St. Nicholas soon would be there;
The children were nestled all snug in their beds,
While visions of sugar-plums danced in their heads;
And mamma in her 'kerchief, and I in my cap,
Had just settled our brains for a long winter's nap,
When out on the lawn there arose such a clatter,
I sprang from my bed to see what was the matter.
Away to the window I flew like a flash,
Tore open the shutters and threw up the sash.
The moon on the breast of the new-fallen snow,
Gave a luster of mid-day to objects below;

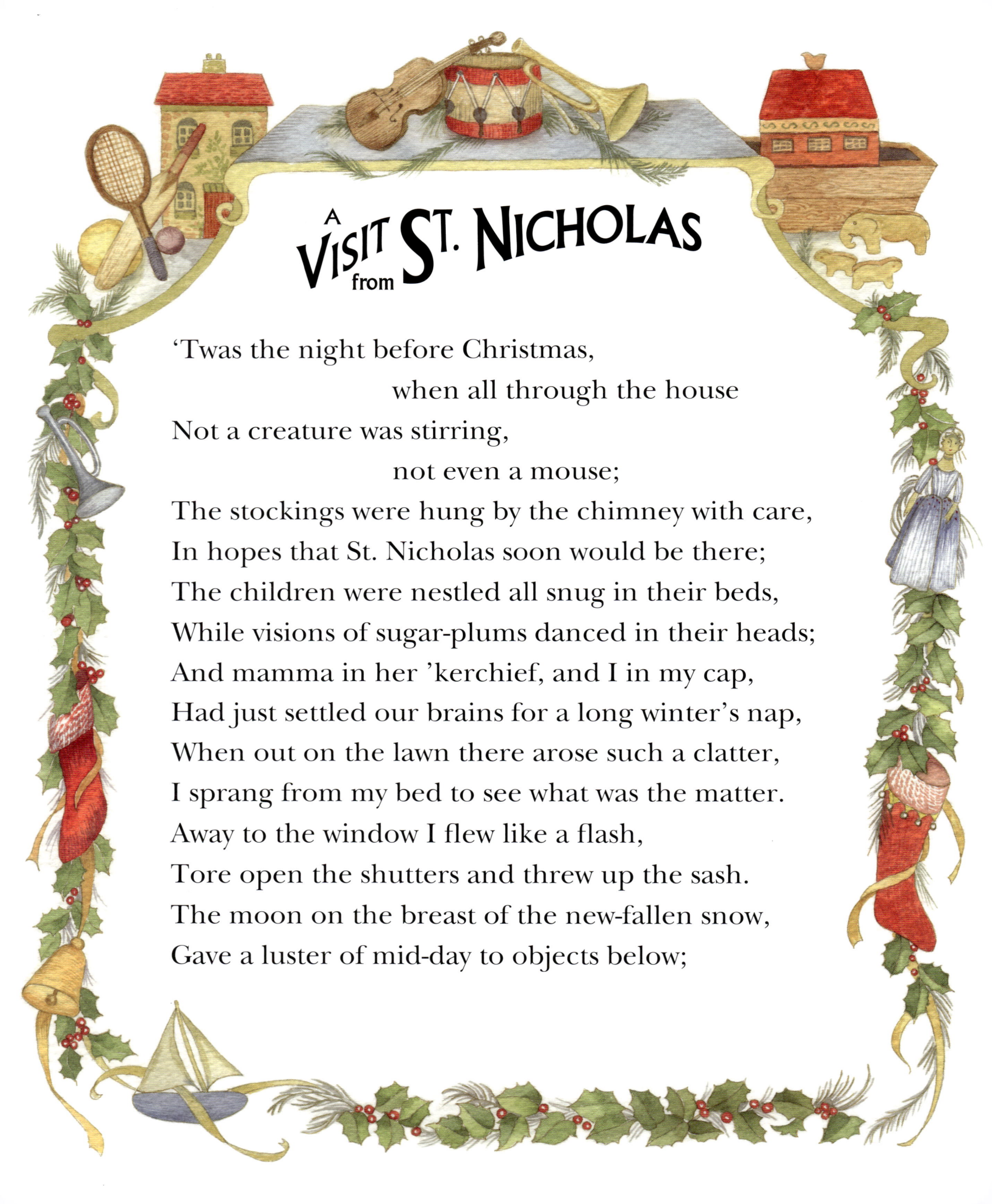

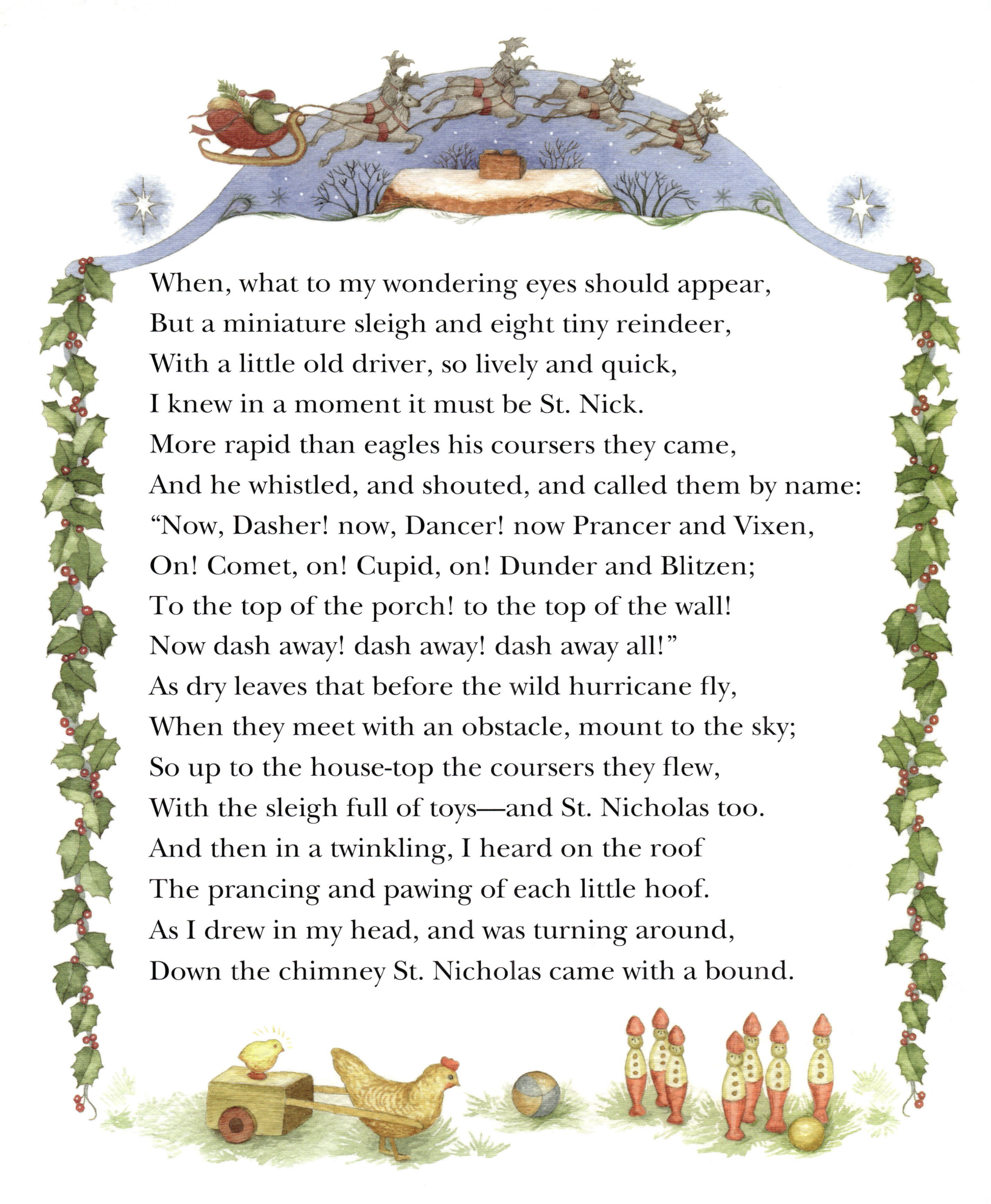

When, what to my wondering eyes should appear,
But a miniature sleigh and eight tiny reindeer,
With a little old driver, so lively and quick,
I knew in a moment it must be St. Nick.
More rapid than eagles his coursers they came,
And he whistled, and shouted, and called them by name:
"Now, Dasher! now, Dancer! now Prancer and Vixen,
On! Comet, on! Cupid, on! Dunder and Blitzen;
To the top of the porch! to the top of the wall!
Now dash away! dash away! dash away all!"
As dry leaves that before the wild hurricane fly,
When they meet with an obstacle, mount to the sky;
So up to the house-top the coursers they flew,
With the sleigh full of toys—and St. Nicholas too.
And then in a twinkling, I heard on the roof
The prancing and pawing of each little hoof.
As I drew in my head, and was turning around,
Down the chimney St. Nicholas came with a bound.

"A MINIATURE SLEIGH AND EIGHT TINY REINDEER."

"DOWN THE CHIMNEY, ST. NICHOLAS CAME."

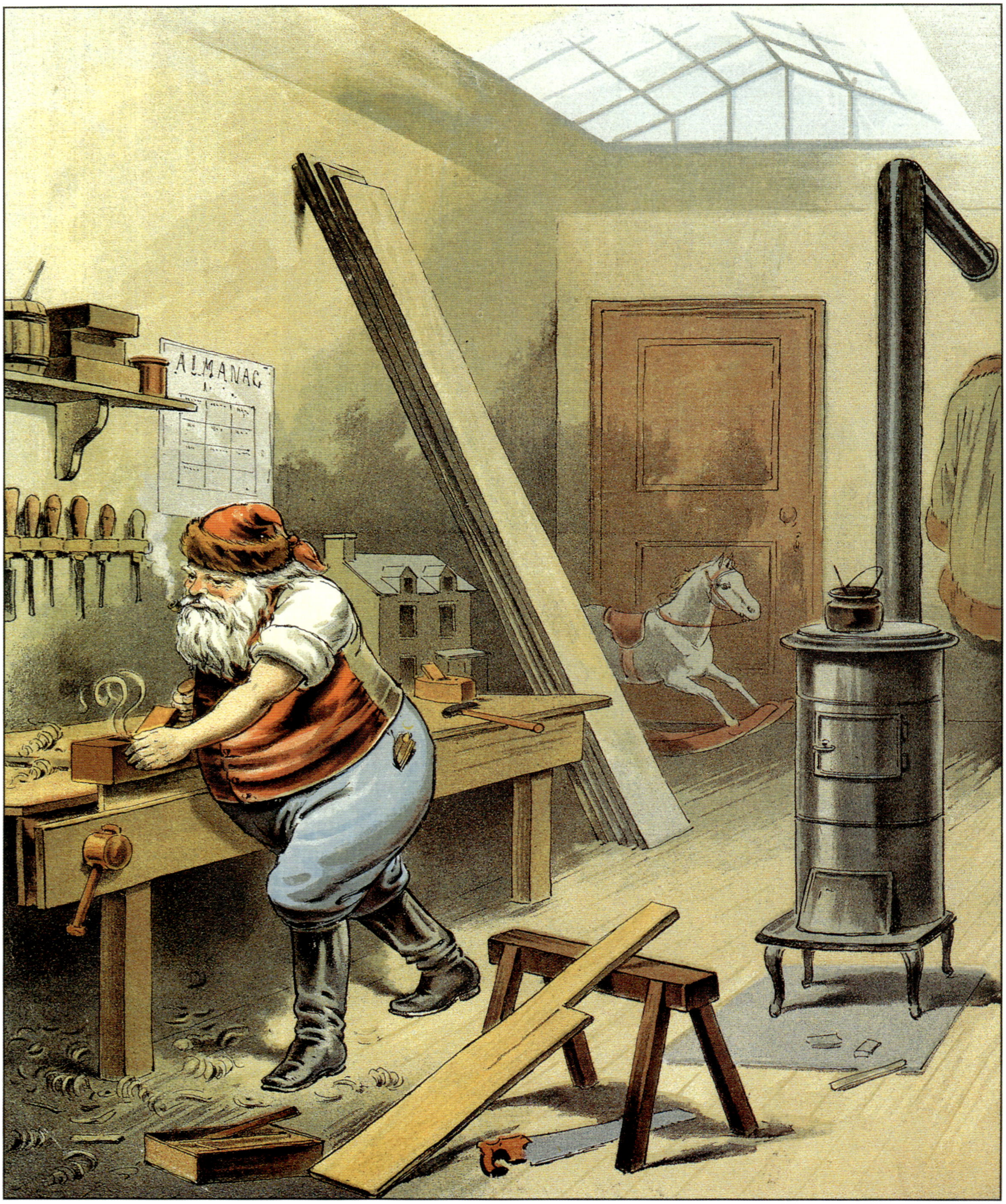
ALMANAC

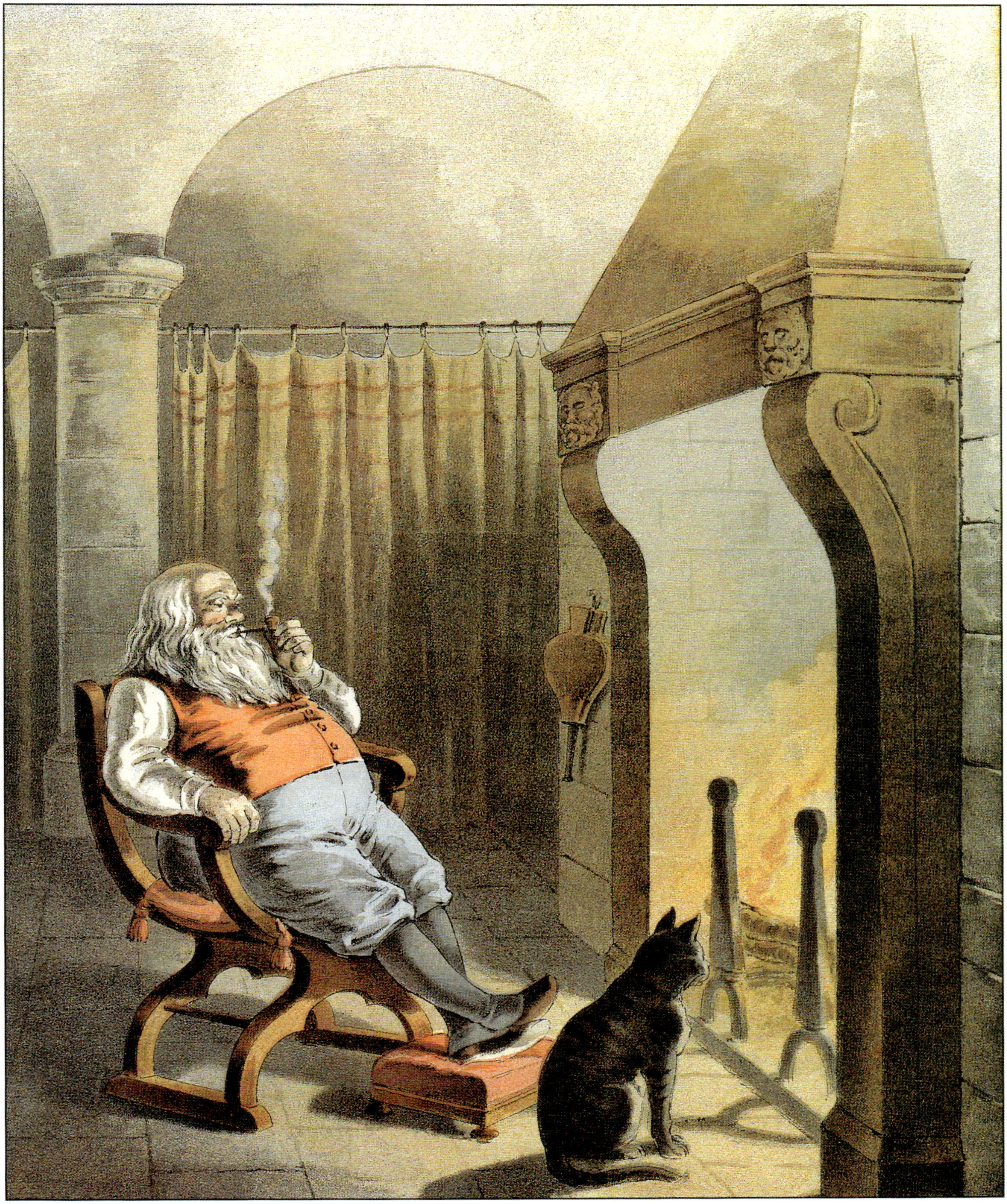

"AND HE WHISTLED, AND SHOUTED, AND CALLED THEM BY
NAME: NOW, DASHER! NOW, DANCER!

NOW, PRANCER AND VIXEN, ON! COMET, ON! CUPID,
ON! DUNDER AND BLITZEN."

He was dressed all in fur,
   from his head to his foot,
And his clothes were all tarnished
   with ashes and soot;
A bundle of toys
   he had flung on his back,
And he looked like a peddler
   just opening his pack.
His eyes—how they twinkled!
   His dimples how merry!
His cheeks were like roses,
   his nose like a cherry;
   His droll little mouth
      was drawn up like a bow,
And the beard on his chin
   was as white as the snow;
The stump of a pipe
   he held tight in his teeth,
And the smoke, it encircled
   his head like a wreath.
He had a broad face
   and a little round belly
That shook when he laughed,
   like a bowl full of jelly.

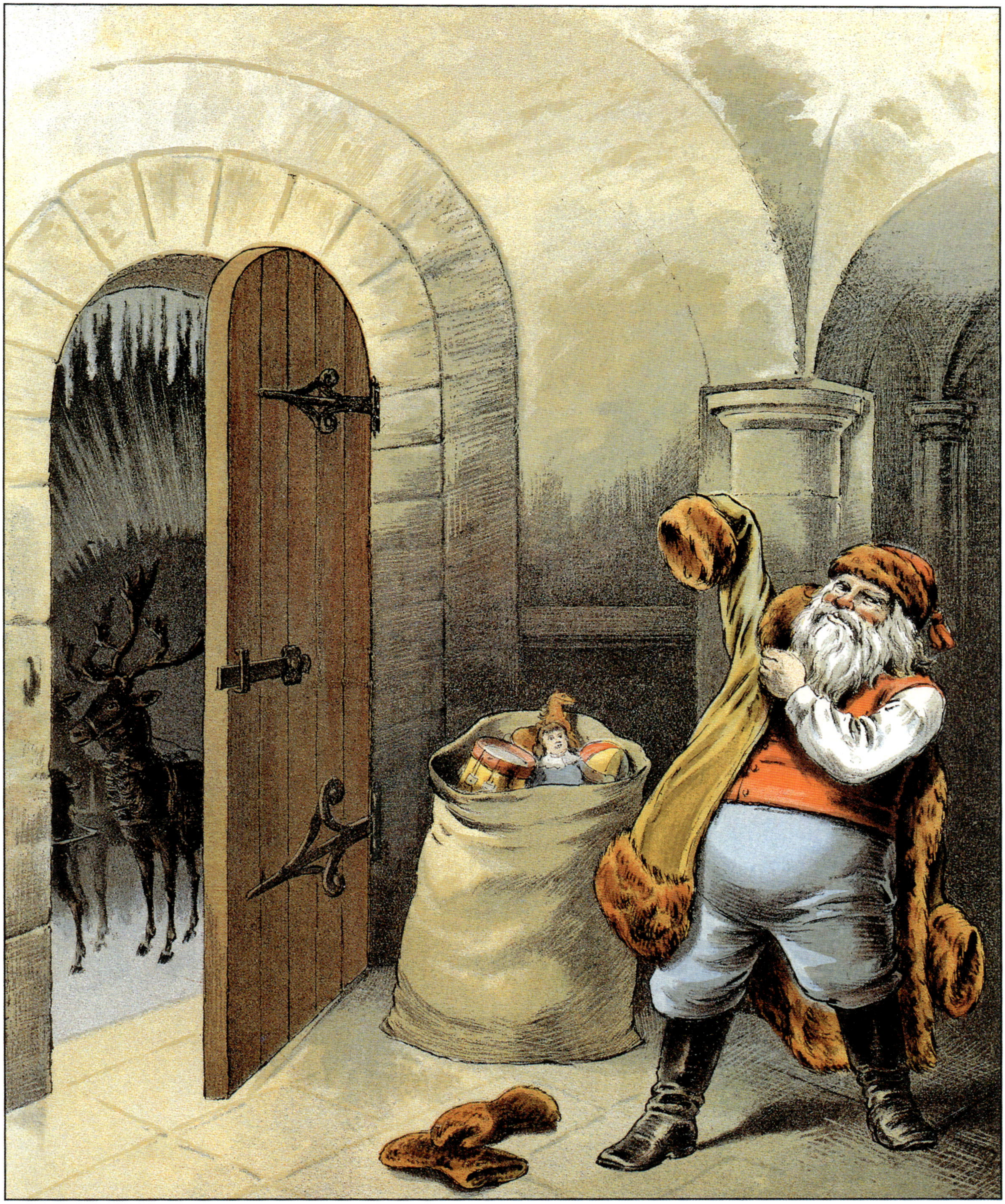

"HE LOOKED LIKE A PEDDLER JUST OPENING HIS PACK."

"HIS EYES—HOW THEY TWINKLED! HIS DIMPLES HOW MERRY!"

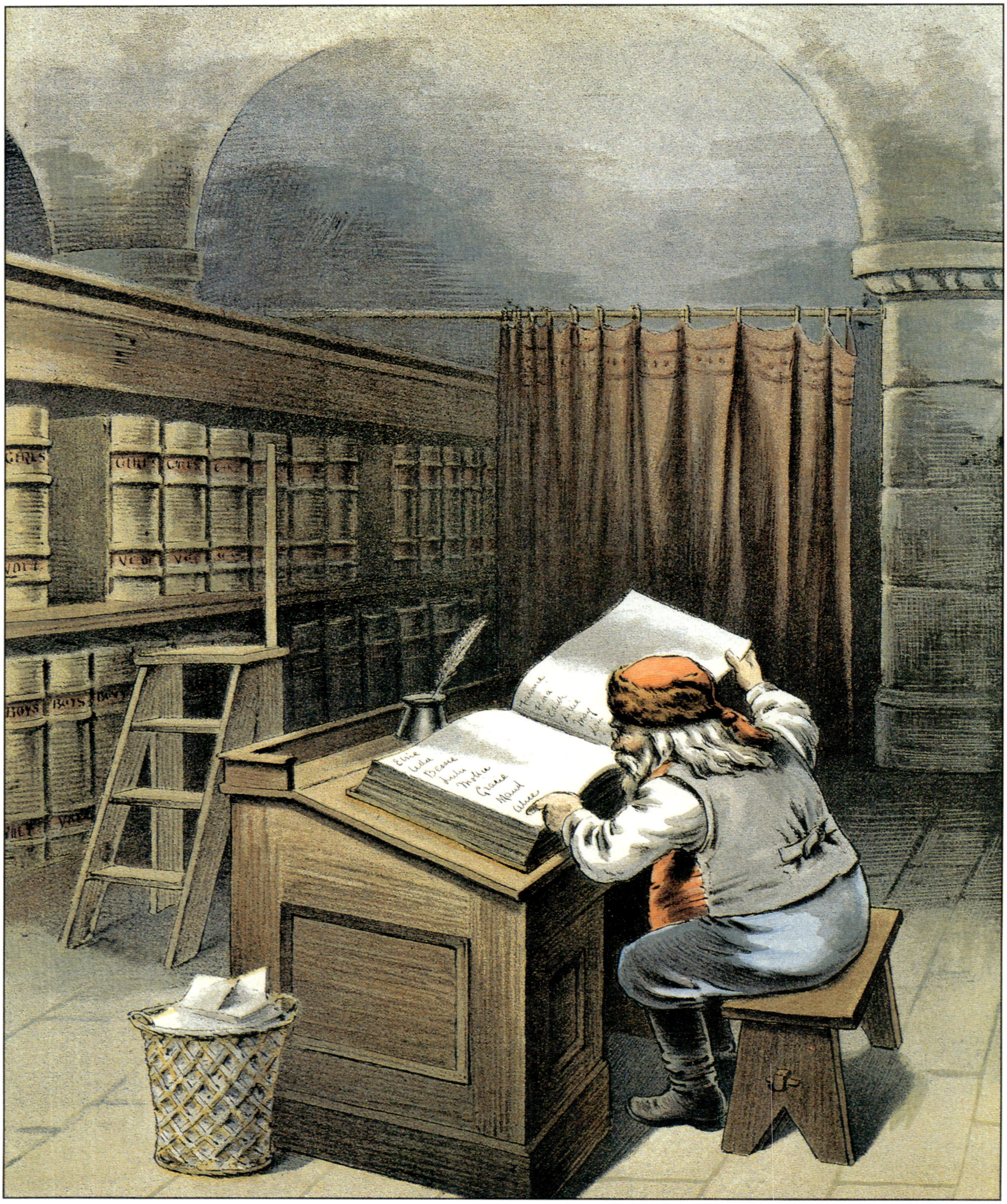

He was chubby and plump,
   a right jolly old elf,
And I laughed when I saw him
   in spite of myself;
A wink of his eye
   and a twist of his head
Soon gave me to know
   I had nothing to dread.
He spoke not a word,
   but went straight to his work,
And filled all the stockings;
   then turned with a jerk,
And laying his finger
   aside of his nose,
And giving a nod,
   up the chimney he rose.
He sprang to his sleigh,
   to his team gave a whistle,
And away they all flew
   like the down of a thistle:
But I heard him exclaim,
   ere he drove out of sight—
"Happy Christmas to all,
   and to all a good night."

"AND FILLED ALL THE STOCKINGS."

"HAPPY CHRISTMAS TO ALL, AND TO ALL A GOOD NIGHT."

This edition is a reproduction of an antique book, published in about 1870. The artwork and the text appear in their original order, with the exception of the illustration on page 2, which appeared on the back cover in the original, and the borders on pages 4, 5, 8, 9, 16, and 21. These have been created by Valerie Greeley in a style imitating the original borders, and show real toys from the nineteenth century. The introduction has also been specially written for this editon.

This edition published in 2021 by Arcturus Publishing Limited
26/27 Bickels Yard, 151–153 Bermondsey Street,
London SE1 3HA

Copyright © Arcturus Holdings Limited

All rights reserved. No part of this publication may be reproduced, stored in a retrieval system, or transmitted, in any form or by any means, electronic, mechanical, photocopying, recording or otherwise, without prior written permission in accordance with the provisions of the Copyright Act 1956 (as amended). Any person or persons who do any unauthorised act in relation to this publication may be liable to criminal prosecution and civil claims for damages.

Introduction by Lisa Regan
Designed by Top Floor Design
Border illustrations by Valerie Greeley
Cover design by Peter Ridley and Jessica Holliland

CH005297US
Supplier 29, Date 0721, Print run 11625

Printed in China